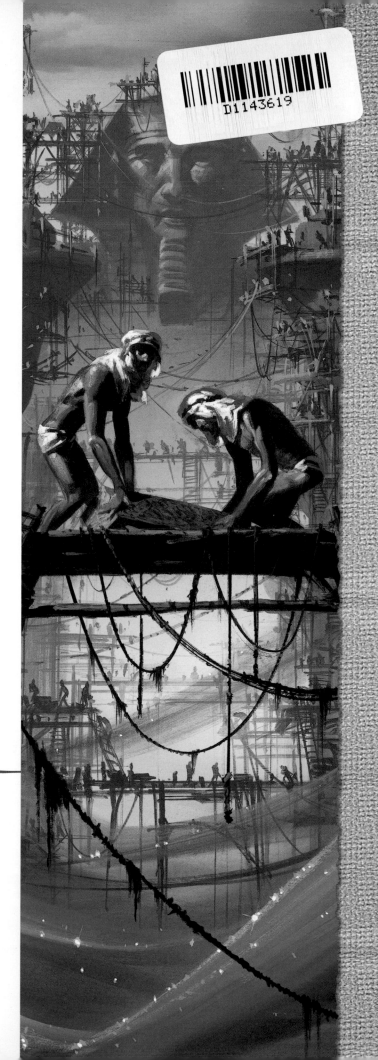

THE PRINCE OF EGYPT

in story and song

with paintings by Kathy Altieri
Richard Chavez
Paul Lasaine
Ron Lukas
Mark Mulgrew
Zhaoping Wei

Introduction

By Stephen Schwartz

I always wanted to be a songwriter. From the time I was a very young child, I used to make up songs. When I was six years old, I asked my parents to buy me a piano. But instead of practising the pieces from my piano lessons, I would fool around making up songs, which certainly annoyed my teacher and my parents as well.

Shortly after we got our piano, my parents took me to see a Broadway musical. It wasn't one you would have heard of, so probably it wasn't very good. But from the moment I saw it, my ambition changed. Now I didn't just want to write songs; I wanted to write songs for musical shows and movies. I wanted to imagine characters and have them sing about how they felt and what they wanted, and I wanted to tell stories using songs to move the plot along.

So my sister and I used to put on puppet shows which we forced our parents to watch. And when I was a bit older, I would beg and bribe and bully my friends into putting on shows with me. We would bore their parents as well as mine!

When I first began writing songs, I actually didn't think about the words very much. As long as they rhymed where they were supposed to and sort of said what the character was feeling, that was okay. But as I got older and more experienced, I began to realize that there were things I deeply cared about and believed in that I wanted to express.

The Prince of Egypt, the story of Moses and the liberation of the Hebrew people from slavery, contains themes and ideas that are important to all people: the responsibility we each have to be true to ourselves, to treat others with respect and decency, and to do what we know is right—no matter how dangerous or difficult. To me this is the essence of morality. It became very important to me that the words to the songs of *The Prince of Egypt* express how I feel about these ideas.

I have been asked what one lyric most expresses the essence of the film to me. I would say that there are two. The first is: "Look at your life through heaven's eyes." It is very easy in this world to judge ourselves by the standards of the society around us: how rich we are, how beautiful or powerful or famous, how good we are at sports or at school. But just as Moses, who was as rich and powerful and privileged as could be, came to realize that these things meant nothing as long as he was being dishonest about who he was and as long as he was allowing others to be enslaved and denied their rights, we each know somewhere inside us that our honesty about ourselves and our actions towards others are what truly count.

The other line that represents to me the essence of *The Prince of Egypt* is: "There can be miracles when you believe." Some believe that God makes miracles for us. Others believe we make our own miracles. In the end, miracles require an act of faith. Faith means that if we believe in and work hard towards our goals, not allowing ourselves to be discouraged or frightened, we can achieve things we never thought possible. For me, the little boy who wanted to be a songwriter and wrote songs for his puppets, to grow up to write songs for *The Prince of Egypt* and be able to share my thoughts and feelings with you seems miraculous indeed.

The other artists represented in this book have achieved their own miracles. All of us hope that in sharing them with you, together we come a little closer to looking at life through heaven's eyes.

Stephen Schwartz
May 1998

Long ago, a powerful Pharaoh ruled the land of Egypt. So that all might see his greatness, he began to build towering monuments and temples in his own likeness. He needed slaves to accomplish this staggering task, and so thousands of Hebrews were pressed into labour under the hot desert sun. As the overseers shouted orders, the Hebrews lifted their voices in a cry of lament.

Deliver Us

MUD—SAND—WATER—

> With the sting of the whip on my shoulder,

STRAW—FASTER!

> With the salt of the sweat on my brow,

LIFT

> Elohim, God on high,

AND PULL

> Can you hear your people cry:

AND RAISE UP—

> Deliver us! Hear our call —

FASTER!

> Deliver us to the Promised Land.

Pharaoh feared the slaves' increasing number. And so he ordered his soldiers to throw all the newborn Hebrew boys into the Nile. But one mother bravely hid her infant child. Covering him in her cloak she ran to the riverbank.

Aaron and Miriam stood guard as their mother carefully placed the baby in a woven basket.
With tears in her eyes, Yocheved sang to her son to calm him as she let the river take him away.

River Lullaby

YAL-DI HA-TOV, VEH HA-RACH
(My good and tender son)

AL TI-RA VEH, AL TIF-CHAD
(Don't be frightened and
don't be scared)

My son, I have nothing I can give
But this chance that you may live.
I pray we'll meet again —

Hush now, my baby.
Be still, love, don't cry.
Sleep as you're rocked by the stream.
Sleep and remember my last lullaby,
So I'll be with you when you dream . . .

Narrowly escaping crocodiles and the flashing nets of fishermen, the basket at last came to the water garden of the palace. When the Queen drew away the lid and discovered a baby inside, she decided the Egyptian gods had sent her a gift. "Come, Rameses," she said to the young prince. "We will show Pharaoh your new baby brother, Moses."

Miriam, who had been watching the whole time, sang her last good-bye:

Brother, you're safe now and safe may you stay,
For I have a prayer just for you:
Grow, baby brother — come back someday.
Come and deliver us, too.

Moses and Rameses were now both princes—princes of Egypt. Proud to be Pharaoh's sons and full of energy, they grew up together, doing everything alike and sometimes careless in their pranks. One day they destroyed a new temple while racing their chariots. Pharaoh was furious, especially with Rameses, his firstborn.

"Do you understand the task for which your birth has destined you?" he asked sternly. "When I pass into the Next World, you will be the morning and evening star. But one weak link can break the chain of this mighty dynasty."

Moses urged Pharaoh to give Rameses another chance. During the royal banquet that night, Pharaoh named Rameses the new prince regent. He would now be responsible for building all the temples.

"And if it pleases you, Father, my first act is to appoint Moses the royal chief architect!" cried Rameses, placing a beautiful scarab ring on his brother's finger.

To the delight of the crowd, the high priests offered the young princes a Midianite captive, but the girl proudly resisted. Without knowing why, Moses allowed her to escape and followed her into the narrow streets of Goshen, where the Hebrews lived.

Moses was watching the Midianite girl hurry toward the desert when he was startled by a pot shattering at his feet. The young woman who dropped the pot seemed to recognize him.

"Oh! I did not expect to see you here . . . of all places . . . at last . . ." She reached to touch him.

It was Miriam, his sister, but Moses did not realize that. "Be careful, slave," he said.

"Our mother set you adrift in a basket to save your life."

"Save my life? From whom?"

"Ask the man you call Father!" Miriam declared. "God saved you to be our deliverer. And you are the deliverer, Moses!"

Now truly angry, Moses turned away. But Miriam began to sing:

Hush now, my baby —

Be still, love, don't cry.

Sleep as you're rocked
by the stream.

Sleep and remember
my last lullaby,

So I'll be with you
when you dream . . .

Moses felt a memory stir, but then he panicked. He raced through the dark streets, the words of the lullaby tearing at his heart, until at last the serene walls of the palace rose before him.

All I Ever Wanted

Gleaming in the moonlight,

Cool and clean and all I've ever known,

All I ever wanted...

Sweet perfumes of incense

Graceful rooms of alabaster stone...

This is my home:

With my father, mother, brother,

Oh so noble, oh so strong!

I am the sovereign prince of Egypt,

A son of the proud history that's shown

Etched on ev'ry wall!

Surely this is all I ever wanted...

Worn out from confusion and emotion, Moses fell asleep and began to dream. But his dream became a nightmare.

In his dream, Moses saw soldiers grab Hebrew babies from the arms of their mothers. He saw his own mother sob as she placed her infant in a basket at the river's edge. Suddenly, he was a Hebrew baby himself, hurtling headfirst into the jaws of a vicious crocodile.

He awoke with a start and ran to look at the paintings on the palace wall. It was true. In the pictures, Egyptian soldiers were tossing babies into the Nile.

"Father," said Moses. "Tell me you didn't do this."

"Oh, my son," said Pharaoh, shaking his head. "They were only slaves."

Early the next morning, the Queen tried to comfort Moses as well.

This is your home, my son.
Here the river brought you . . .
Now forget and be content.
When the gods send you a blessing,
You don't ask why it was sent.

But Moses could find no comfort with her, nor with his brother Rameses, who was ecstatic about his plans for building a new monument.

"Throughout all time to come, men shall gaze upon this temple and say, 'It was the great Rameses who built this!'" he said proudly.

Moses scarcely could see the plans or hear his brother's words. Instead he saw the suffering of each Hebrew slave. Instead he heard the loud cracking of the whip as a guard beat an old man.

When he could stand it no longer, he jumped up and yelled at the guard to stop. They struggled on the scaffolding, but the guard lost his footing and fell to his death. Then Moses fled.

"Wait!" said Rameses, trying to catch him. "I say you are innocent."

"What you say does not matter," said Moses sadly. "Good-bye, Brother."

Moses was a tiny figure in the vast desert. Blazing days passed into frigid nights. Away from friends, palaces, and possessions, all that had been Egypt was lost to him. He cast away his sandals and wig, and all his ornaments—except the scarab ring. He stumbled aimlessly, with nothing to eat or drink, until one day a severe storm swept over the desert. As the harsh sand stung his eyelids and the crying voice of the wind echoed in his ears, he sank to his knees. Soon the sands had covered him completely.

Finally, a curious camel came by. With his last bit of strength, Moses grabbed on to the camel's rope and was dragged through the desert to a well.

While Moses was eagerly drinking, he heard a cry. A rough band of men had fallen upon three young girls and their sheep. Moses drove the brigands' camels far off into the desert. Soon he discovered that the girls were the sisters of Tzipporah, the young woman he had followed from the palace. Their father was Jethro, the high priest of Midian.

Later that night, Jethro honoured his guest with a feast. When Moses declared himself unworthy of honour, Jethro tried to persuade him to look at life in a new way.

Through Heaven's Eyes

A single thread in a tapestry—

Though its colour brightly shine—

Can never see its purpose

In the pattern of the grand design.

And the stone that sits on the very top

Of the mountain's mighty face—

Does it think it's more important

Than the stones that form the base?

Years passed. Moses began to appreciate his new
life as a shepherd. He learned to love the sky and
rejoice in the laughter of children. He began to
celebrate all people, especially Tzipporah.

No life can escape being blown about

By the winds of change and chance,

And though you never know all the steps,

You must learn to join the dance . . .

One night as the villagers feasted, Tzipporah held out her hand to Moses and he accepted it. He was ready to join the circle at last.

With great sunlight in his heart, he joined the dancers and held Tzipporah close to him. They danced and danced . . . and decided to become man and wife.

So how do you judge what a man is worth?

By what he builds or buys?

You can never see with your eyes on earth—

Look at your life

Through heaven's eyes!

One morning, Moses followed a sheep into a canyon and discovered a strange sight. Before him was a bush that burned yet was not consumed. When he put his hand in the fire, he felt no pain. Then a voice whispered his name.

"Moses... Moses... Moses... Moses..."

"Here I am," replied Moses.

*"Take the shoes from off your feet, for the place
on which you stand is holy ground."*

Moses slowly did as he was told. "Who are you?"

*"I am that I am. I am the God of your ancestors:
Abraham, Isaac, and Jacob."*

"What do you want with me?" said Moses, hiding his face.

*"I have seen the oppression of my people in Egypt
and have heard their cry. So I have come down to deliver
them out of slavery and bring them to their promised land.
And so unto Pharaoh I shall send you."*

"Me? Who am I?" said Moses, falling to his knees. "I was their enemy."

*"Who made man's mouth? Who made the deaf, the mute,
the seeing or the blind? Did not I? Now go!"*

Then God took pity on Moses, sending a gentle wind to caress his skin.

*"Oh, Moses, I shall be with you when you go
to the King of Egypt. But Pharaoh will not listen.
So I will stretch out my hand and smite Egypt
with all my wonders. Take the staff in your hand,
Moses...With it, you shall do my wonders."*

There was silence. Moses looked up in awe. The bush no longer burned but now flowered.

oses rushed to tell Tzipporah of the great task set before him.

"Look at your family," he said. "They are free. That is what I want for my people. And that is why I must do the task that God has given me."

And so Moses and Tzipporah returned together to Egypt. As they made their way towards the palace, Moses saw that the monuments were larger and the suffering was greater than he had remembered.

When Moses at last entered the throne room, he was shocked to see that his brother Rameses was now Pharaoh. Rameses was overjoyed to see Moses, until he heard the message his brother had brought.

"The God of the Hebrews commands that you let them go."

"Commands?" asked Rameses, amused.

"Behold the power of God!" declared Moses.

Moses threw his staff on the ground. It became a twisting, writhing snake. But Rameses was not impressed. He called forth his own magicians to answer Moses.

Hotep and Huy closed their eyes and began to chant.

MUT...

NEKHBET...

SOKAR... SELKET...

ANUKIS...

SESHMU...

MESHKENT...

So you think you've got friends in high places
With the power to put us on the run.
Well, forgive us these smiles on our faces,
You'll know what power is when we're done . . .

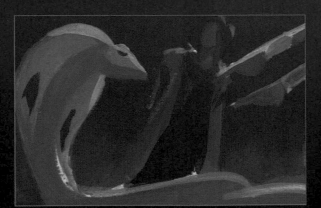

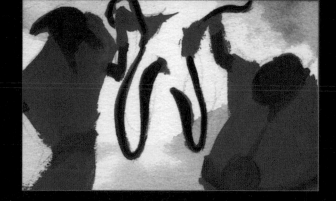

You're playing with the big boys now...

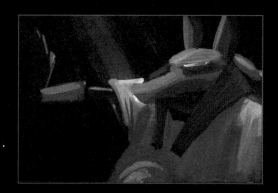

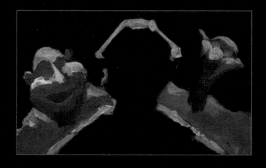

Stop this foolish mission—

Watch a true magician—

Pick up your silly twig, boy...

You're playing with the big boys now!

hey threw down their rods. Sinister snakes surrounded Moses.

The crowd cheered, and Hotep and Huy proudly took their bows. But there was something everyone failed to see

In the shadows, Moses' snake devoured Hotep and Huy's snakes.

When Rameses realized that his brother had only returned to free the Hebrews, his heart became hardened.

"I do not know this God, neither will I let your people go," he said. "Tell your people their workload has been doubled."

Utterly dejected, Moses might have given up, had not his sister pleaded with him.

"God saved you in all your wanderings," she said. "Even now God will not abandon you. So don't you abandon us."

Inspired by her words, Moses rose to his feet like a mighty oak. He walked to the edge of the Nile and thrust his staff into the water. Immediately, the blue waters began to turn to blood. Rameses' guards yelled with terror and tried to get back to the royal barge.

Even the Hebrews grew frightened, but Moses stood firm.

"Pharaoh can take away your food, your homes, your freedom. He can take away your sons and daughters. With one word, Pharaoh can take away your very lives," he said.

"But there is one thing he cannot take away from you—your faith."

The Plagues

Thus saith the Lord:

Since you refuse to free my people

All through the land of Egypt...

I send a pestilence and plague

Into your house, into your bed

Into your streams, into your streets

Into your drink, into your bread

Until you break, until you yield!

And God sent plague after plague to Egypt.
With each plague, Moses' heart grew
heavier, but still Pharaoh would not relent.

{Moses}

Once I called you brother.

Once I thought the chance to make you laugh

Was all I ever wanted...

And even now I wish that God had chosen another.

Serving as your foe on his behalf

Is the last thing that I wanted.

{Rameses}

You who I called brother—

How could you have come to hate me so?

Is this what you wanted?...

Then let my heart be hardened,

And never mind how high the cost may grow—

This will still be so:

I will never let your people go!

{Moses}

Let my people go!

A plague of darkness fell upon Egypt. Temples that had once stood proudly beneath the Egyptian sun slowly crumpled under its weight.

Moses pleaded with Pharaoh one last time. But Rameses, bitterly prideful, spoke the words that would give form to the final plague.

"My father had the right idea. And it's about time I finished the job...There will be a great cry in all of Egypt, such as has never been heard nor will be again!"

Moses knew that God would answer Rameses' terrible promise.

Returning to Goshen, he spoke to his people.

"The Lord has spoken to me again, saying, 'You must take a lamb, and with its blood, mark the lintel of every door. For tonight I shall pass through the land of Egypt and smite all the firstborn. But when I see the mark upon your door, I will pass over you, and the plague shall not enter.'"

And so it was done.

That night, the angel of death passed over the marked doors of the Hebrews. But softly exhaling, it stole the last breath of every firstborn Egyptian child. No one was spared—not even Pharaoh's beloved son. And a great cry sounded throughout Egypt.

Moses entered the palace and found Rameses standing over the lifeless body of his son.

"You and your people have my permission to go," he said.

With deep sorrow and compassion, Moses reached out and laid his hand on Rameses' shoulder.

"Leave me!"

Outside the palace, Moses wept.

Tzipporah saw her husband's anguish and embraced him. But Miriam lifted her voice in song. Finally, the long days of lamentation were over.

When You Believe

Many nights we've prayed
With no proof anyone could hear.
In our hearts a hopeful song
We barely understood.
Now we are not afraid—
Although we know there's much to fear.
We were moving mountains
Long before we knew we could!

One by one, the former slaves walked as free men, women, and children through the streets of Goshen, gathering confidence at each step.

Moses led the crowd, with Tzipporah and Miriam by his side. Into the desert they marched, and their newfound joy gradually spilled over into song and celebration.

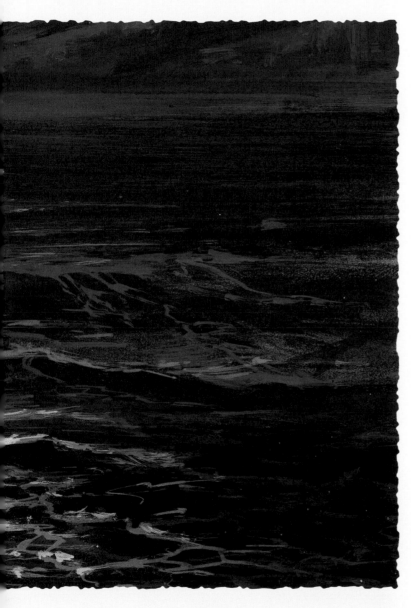

In this time of fear,

When prayer so often proved in vain,

Hope seemed like the summer birds

Too swiftly flown away.

Yet now I'm standing here

With heart so full I can't explain,

Seeking faith and speaking words

I never thought I'd say:

There can be miracles

When you believe!

Days later, as the Hebrews neared the Red Sea, Rameses' army suddenly appeared. Pharaoh had changed his mind.

But God did not abandon them. A pillar of fire burst from the water, blocking the army's path. Then Moses walked to the edge of the sea. He lifted his staff and turned his eyes to heaven. God spoke to Moses . . .

With this staff, you shall do my wonders.

The Hebrews entered the parted sea. Between the walls of water they made their way over

mud and rock. Then the pillar of fire sank into the ground, and Rameses ordered his army to

charge into the divide. But when Pharaoh's charioteers tried to pass through, the turbulent waters

closed over them. Rameses' mighty army was lost; he stood alone on the shore. On the opposite

side of the sea, Moses stared back across the waters and said a last good-bye to the man who had

been his brother.

The Hebrews were triumphant. God had heard their cry and had saved them yet again. Now

their voices rang out in joy as they began their journey to the Promised Land.

Finally, they were free.

Send a shepherd to shepherd us—

And deliver us to the Promised Land.

Deliver us!

Deliver Us

EGYPTIAN GUARDS

Mud…Sand…Water…Straw…Faster!
Mud…And lift…Sand…And pull
Water…And raise up…Straw…Faster!

HEBREW SLAVES

With the sting of the whip on my shoulder,
With the salt of my sweat on my brow,
Elohim, God on high,
Can you hear your people cry:
Help us now
This dark hour…

Deliver us!
Hear our call.
Deliver us,
Lord of all.
Remember us, here in this burning sand.
Deliver us!
There's a land you promised us—
Deliver us to the Promised Land…

YOCHEVED

Yal-di ha-tov, veh ha-rach,
(My good and tender son,)
Al ti-ra veh, al tif-chad.
(Don't be frightened and don't be scared.)
My son, I have nothing I can give
But this chance that you may live.
I pray we'll meet again
If he will deliver us…

HEBREW SLAVES

Deliver us!
Hear our prayer.
Deliver us
From despair.
These years of slavery grow too cruel to stand.
Deliver us!
There's a land you promised us—
Deliver us
Out of bondage and

Deliver us to the Promised Land…

YOCHEVED

Hush now, my baby,
Be still, love, don't cry.
Sleep as you're rocked by the stream.
Sleep and remember
My last lullaby
So I'll be with you when you dream.

River, O river,
Flow gently for me,
Such precious cargo you bear.
Do you know somewhere
He can live free?
River, deliver him there…

YOUNG MIRIAM

Brother, you're safe now
And safe may you stay,
For I have a prayer just for you:
Grow, baby brother,
Come back someday,
Come and deliver us, too…

HEBREW SLAVES

Deliver us!
Send a shepherd to shepherd us
And deliver us to the Promised Land,
Deliver us to the Promised Land.

YOCHEVED

Deliver us!

All I Ever Wanted

MOSES

Gleaming in the moonlight,
Cool and clean and all I've ever known,
All I ever wanted.
Sweet perfumes of incense,
Graceful rooms of alabaster stone,
All I ever wanted.

This is my home:
With my father, mother, brother,
Oh so noble, oh so strong!
Now I am home.
Here among my trappings and belongings
I belong,
And if anybody doubts it,
They couldn't be more wrong.

I am a sovereign prince of Egypt,
A son of the proud history that's shown
Etched on ev'ry wall!
Surely this is all I ever wanted,
All I ever wanted,
All I ever wanted.

QUEEN

This is your home, my son.
Here the river brought you,
And it's here the river meant

To be your home.
Now you know the truth, love,
Now forget and be content.
When the gods send you a blessing
You don't ask why it was sent…

Through Heaven's Eyes

JETHRO

A single thread in a tapestry—
Though its colour brightly shine—
Can never see its purpose
In the pattern of the grand design.

And the stone that sits on the very top
Of the mountain's mighty face—
Does it think it's more important
Than the stones that form the base?

So how can you see what your life is worth
Or where your value lies?
You can never see through the eyes of man—
You must look at your life,
Look at your life through heaven's eyes.
Lai-la-lai…

A lake of gold in the desert sand
Is less than a cool fresh spring—
And to one lost sheep, a shepherd boy
Is greater than the richest king.
If a man lose ev'rything he owns,
Has he truly lost his worth?
Or is it the beginning
Of a new and brighter birth?

So how do you measure the worth of a man—
In wealth or strength or size?
In how much he gained or how much he gave?
The answer will come,
The answer will come to him who tries
To look at his life through heaven's eyes.

And that's why we share all we have with you,
Though there's little to be found.
When all you've got is nothing,
There's a lot to go around.

No life can escape being blown about
By the winds of change and chance,

And though you never know all the steps,
You must learn to join the dance—
You must learn to join the dance.
Lai-la-lai...

So how do you judge what a man is worth?
By what he builds or buys?
You can never see with your eyes on earth—
Look through heaven's eyes.
Look at your life,
Look at your life,
Look at your life through heaven's eyes!

Playing with the Big Boys

HOTEP AND HUY

By the power of Ra...
Mut...Nut...Khnum...Ptah...
Nephthys...Nekhbet...Sobek...Sekhmet...
Sokar...Selket...Reshpu...Wadjet...
Anubis...Anukis...
Seshmu...Meshkent...Hemsut...Tefnut...
Heket...Mafdet...
Ra...Mut...Nut...Ptah...
Hemsut...Tefnut...Sokar...Selket...
Seshmu...Reshpu...Sobek...Wadjet...
Heket...Mafdet...Nephthys...Nekhbet...Ra...

So you think you've got friends in high places
With the power to put us on the run.
Well, forgive us these smiles on our faces,
You'll know what power is when we are done,
Son...

You're playing with the big boys now,
Playing with the big boys now.
Ev'ry spell and gesture
Tells you who's the best, you're
Playing with the big boys now.

You're playing with the big boys now,
You're playing with the big boys now.
Stop this foolish mission—
Watch a true magician
Give an exhibition how.
Pick up your silly twig, boy,
You're playing with the big boys now!

EGYPTIAN PRIESTS

By the power of Ra,
Mut, Nut, Khnum, Ptah,
Sobek, Sekhmet, Sokar, Selket,
Anubis, Anukis,

Hemsut, Tefnut, Meshkent, Mafdet...

HOTEP AND HUY

You're playing with the big boys now,
You're playing with the big boys now.
By the might of Horus,
You will kneel before us—
Kneel to our splendorous power...
You put up a front,
You put up a fight,
And just to show we feel no spite,
You can be our acolyte.
But first, boy, it's time to bow
(Kowtow!)
Or it's your own grave you'll dig, boy.
You're playing with the big boys,
Playing with the big boys
Now!

The Plagues

CHORUS

Thus saith the Lord:
Since you refuse to free my people
All through the land of Egypt...

I send a pestilence and plague
Into your house, into your bed,
Into your streams, into your streets,
Into your drink, into your bread,
Upon your cattle, on your sheep,
Upon your oxen in your field,
Into your dreams, into your sleep,
Until you break, until you yield,
I send the swarm, I send the horde,
Thus saith the Lord.

MOSES

Once I called you brother—
Once I thought the chance to make you laugh
Was all I ever wanted...

CHORUS

I send the thunder from the sky,
I send the fire raining down.

MOSES

And even now I wish that God had chosen another—
Serving as your foe on his behalf
Is the last thing that I wanted...

CHORUS

I send a hail of burning ice
On ev'ry field, on ev'ry town.

MOSES

This was my home.
All this pain and devastation,
How it tortures me inside—
All the innocent who suffer
From your stubbornness and pride...

CHORUS

I send the locusts on a wind
Such as the world has never seen—
On ev'ry leaf, on ev'ry stalk,
Until there's nothing left of green.
I send my scourge, I send my sword,
Thus saith the Lord!

MOSES

You who I called brother,
Why must you call down another blow?

CHORUS

I send my scourge, I send my sword...

MOSES

Let my people go.

MOSES AND CHORUS

Thus saith the Lord.

RAMESES

You who I called brother,
How could you have come to hate me so?
Is this what you wanted?

CHORUS

I send the swarm, I send the horde...

RAMESES

Then let my heart be hardened
And never mind how high the cost may grow—
This will still be so:
I will never let your people go...

CHORUS

Thus saith the Lord:

MOSES

Thus saith the Lord:

RAMESES

I will not...

MOSES, RAMESES, AND CHORUS

Let your (my) people go!

When You Believe

MIRIAM

Many nights we've prayed
With no proof anyone could hear—
In our hearts a hopeful song
We barely understood.
Now we are not afraid—
Although we know there's much to fear.

We were moving mountains
Long before we knew we could!

There can be miracles
When you believe—
Though hope is frail,
It's hard to kill.

Who knows what miracles
You can achieve
When you believe
Somehow you will,
You will when you believe.

TZIPPORAH

In this time of fear,
When prayer so often proved in vain,
Hope seemed like the summer birds
Too swiftly flown away.
Yet now I'm standing here
With heart so full I can't explain,
Seeking faith and speaking words
I never thought I'd say.

MIRIAM AND TZIPPORAH

There can be miracles
When you believe—
Though hope is frail,
It's hard to kill.
Who knows what miracles
You can achieve
When you believe
Somehow you will,
You will when you believe.

HEBREW CHILDREN

A-shi-ra l'a-don-ai ki ga-oh ga-ah
(I will sing to the Lord, for he has triumphed gloriously)

A-shi-ra l'a-don-ai ki ga-oh ga-ah
(I will sing to the Lord, for he has triumphed gloriously)

Mi-cha-mo-cha ba-elim adonai
(Who is like you, oh Lord, among the celestial)

Mi-ka-mo-cha ne-dar- ba-ko-desh
(Who is like you, majestic in holiness)

Na-chi-tah v'-chas-d'-cha am zu ga-al-ta
(In your love, you lead the people you redeemed)

Na-chi-tah v'-chas-d'-cha am zu ga-al-ta
(In your love, you lead the people you redeemed)

A-shi-ra, a-shi-ra, a-shi-ra ...

(I will sing, I will sing, I will sing...)

HEBREWS

There can be miracles
When you believe—
Though hope is frail,
It's hard to kill.
Who knows what miracles
You can achieve
When you believe
Somehow you will—
Now you will,
You will when you believe.

MIRIAM AND TZIPPORAH

You will when you believe.

River Lullaby

Hush now, my baby,
Be still, love, don't cry.
Sleep as you're rocked by the stream—
Sleep and remember
My last lullaby,
So I'll be with you when you dream.

Drift on a river
That flows through my arms,
Drift as I'm singing to you.
I see you smiling,
So peaceful and calm—
And holding you, I'm smiling too—
Here in my arms.
Safe from all harm.
Holding you, I'm smiling too.

Lu lu lu lu lu lu lu
Lu lu lu lu lu lu lu

Hush now, my baby,
Be still, love, don't cry.
Sleep as you're rocked by the stream—
Sleep and remember this river lullaby,
So I'll be with you when you dream—
I'll be with you when you dream.

PUFFIN BOOKS

Published by the Penguin Group: Penguin Books Ltd, Registered Offices:
Harmondsworth, Middlesex, England

First published in the USA by Dutton Children's Books 1998
Published in Puffin Books 1998
10 9 8 7 6 5 4 3 2 1
TM & © DreamWorks, 1998
All rights reserved

Paintings by Kathy Altieri, Richard Chavez, Paul Lasaine, Ron Lukas,
Mark Mulgrew, and Zhaoping Wei.
Text adapted by Nancy Shayne.
Lyrics and introduction by Stephen Schwartz.
Art direction by Rick Farley.
Designed by Rhion Magee.

The music for *The Prince of Egypt* commemorates a first-time collaboration
by two Academy Award®-winners. The score and songs for the original motion
picture soundtrack were produced and arranged by Hans Zimmer, with music
and lyrics by Stephen Schwartz.